MAKING YOUR OWN GOURMET COFFEE DRINKS

MAKING
YOUR OWN
GOURMET
COFFEE
DRINKS

Espressos,
Cappuccinos,
Lattes,
Mochas,
and More!

Mathew Tekulsky

Illustrations by Clair Moritz

Crown Publishers, Inc.
New York

To Brandt Aymar

Published by Crown Publishers, Inc.,
201 East 50th Street, New York, New York 10022.
Member of the Crown Publishing Group.

Random House, Inc. New York, Toronto, London, Sydney, Auckland
http://www.randomhouse.com/

CROWN and colophon are trademarks of Crown Publishers, Inc.

Printed in the United States of America

Book design by Nancy Kenmore

Library of Congress Cataloging-in-Publication Data
Tekulsky, Mathew.
Making your own gourmet coffee drinks / by Mathew Tekulsky.—1st ed.
Includes index.
1. Coffee. 2. Espresso. I. Title.
TX817.C6T45   1993
641.6'373—dc20   91-44895

ISBN 0-517-58824-2

15 14 13 12

Acknowledgments

I would like to thank the following for their generous assistance in the writing of this book: Barnie's Coffee & Tea Company, Gloria Jean's Gourmet Coffees, Green Mountain Coffee Roasters, and Starbucks Coffee Company. Thanks as well to the Robert Bosch Corpora-tion, Melitta, the Pasquini Espres- so Company, and Toddy Prod- ucts for their help. Thanks, as always, to my literary agent, Jane Jordan Browne, for her continued sup- port, and to my editor, Brandt Aymar, for his great advice. Finally, I wish to thank the friendly coffee servers at the many gourmet coffee shops that I visited during the course of writing this book. Their generous sharing of information on recipes and how certain drinks are made is greatly appreciated.

Contents

Introduction
9

Hot Drinks Made with Brewed Coffee

Introduction

For centuries, people have been enjoying coffee. From the Arabian and Turkish coffeehouses of the sixteenth century, on through the explosion of London's coffeehouses in the seventeenth century, citizens of the world have been brought together by their shared love of this tasty and uplifting bever- age, as well as the charming companionship of like-minded friends. Even though coffeehouses ex- isted in Colo- nial America, it wasn't until af- ter the Boston Tea Party that coffee really became the national drink—which it has remained ever since. In the past few years, however, there has been a dramatic increase in the popularity of specialty coffee shops in the United States. Whereas people were once just inter- ested in having a standard cup of coffee, now they not only enjoy a regular espresso or cappuccino at the coffee bar, they're also *ordering specialty drinks with names such as Cappuccino Royale, Espresso con Panna, Mochaccino, and Latte Macchiato. And like wine connoisseurs, they are choosing coffee beans for home use with such names as Colombian Supremo, Ethiopian Harrar, Kona, and Jamaican Blue Mountain. Various specialty coffee shops also have their own house blends, or they may call a certain blend Gazebo, Andes Blend, or Swedish Supreme.*

With this book, you will not only learn how to brew a great cup of gourmet coffee at home,

using a variety of techniques, you will also discover how to incorporate this coffee into many of the most delicious gourmet coffee drinks that are being served in the best specialty coffee shops around the country today. And you will learn how to make many traditional coffee drinks that have been popular for generations. In addition, once you have tried the recipes included here, you will probably want to experiment on your own with different ingredients, depending on your own tastes. You may even come up with a few new gourmet coffee drinks!

The Various Coffee Beans
You Can Use

Before we start making drinks, we should learn a little bit about the various beans you can use, the type of equipment available for making coffee, and a few other useful tips that will help you do such things as keep your coffee fresh, grind the beans for maximum usability, steam your milk properly for cappuccinos, and prepare your iced coffee the right way.

Coffee comes from the seed of a coffee plant, which is processed and then roasted according to various specifications. The best coffee in the world comes from the *Coffea arabica* plant, which grows at high altitudes throughout the equatorial regions of the world.

Originally discovered growing wild in Ethiopia in ancient times, this plant was taken to Yemen by the Arabs and cultivated there as early as the sixth century. In the early 1700s, the Dutch began cultivating descendants of these original plants in Java, and from that time on, the cultivation of the *C. arabica* plant spread to many areas of Central America, South America, and Africa.

Another species of coffee plant, *Coffea robusta,* is also grown commercially (primarily in Africa), but this plant is used mostly for the lower grades of coffee that are on the market today.

Depending on where in the world your coffee is grown—from Indonesia to Central and South America, to Africa and the Middle East—it will have its own distinct taste and body. Coffee from Java, for instance, is earthy tasting and full-bodied, while beans from Costa Rica produce a lighter, more tangy cup of coffee. Columbian and Brazilian coffees are more middle-of-the-road types, providing a mild taste that can easily be blended with other beans. Coffee from Kenya, on the other hand, has a strong, winy taste.

Indeed, coffee from various regions of the same country will have its own unique flavor, depending on such factors as altitude, rainfall, and soil quality—and coffee from different plantations within the same region will even taste different from each other. Therefore, today's specialty coffee wholesalers and retailers send coffee tasters all over the world in search of the best-tasting coffee crop from each region.

After the green coffee beans are shipped to the United States, they must be roasted. This involves heating the beans at around 400°F. for about 5 to 15 minutes (depending on the temperature), while rotating them in large bins.

Most beans are light or medium roasted, producing a light- or medium-brown color and mild taste. Viennese or dark-roasted coffee produces a darker brown bean and an almost burnt (yet tangy) taste. The darkest roast (called espresso, Italian, or French) has a dark brown to almost black color and a burnt to charcoaly taste.

Coffee beans can also be blended to create desired effects. The combination of Mocha (a mild bean from Yemen) and Java, for instance, has become synonymous with the coffee drink itself. Other blends use a variety of different-tasting beans from various parts of the world, along with a variety of roasts. Hence, an excellent morning-coffee blend might include a majority of Viennese-roasted beans, along with half as much Mocha and a little bit of espresso roast just to spice things up. A good after-dinner blend, on the other hand, might include 50 percent Mocha-Java along with 25 percent each of Colombian and Costa Rican.

The proliferation of specialty coffee shops over the last few years has produced another new trend—that of flavored coffee beans. Thus, you'll find names such as Vanilla Nut, Chocolate Almond, and Irish Cream labeling bags of specially weighed and packaged coffees at your local shop (or you can order them by mail from the sources listed in the directory at the end of this book). Of course, you can always add flavorings or extracts to regular unflavored coffee after it's brewed, as the recipes that follow will indicate. Conversely, you may wish to use flavored coffees in any of the following recipes, being careful not to mix tastes that don't go together well.

In recent years, the quality of decaffeinated coffee has been rising significantly—at least on the gourmet level. Whereas in the past, lower-quality beans were commonly used for decaffeinated varieties, today there is no reason why you can't find a good-tasting decaffeinated coffee at a specialty coffee shop or elsewhere.

There are two basic types of decaffeination processes: one uses a solvent (most commonly methylene chloride) that clings to the caffeine and is then flushed away; another (the Swiss water process) uses repeated flushings of water to wash away the caffeine. The first process is generally acknowledged to produce a better-tasting cup of coffee (with virtually no chemical residue), while the Swiss water process is becoming increasingly popular because it uses no chemicals.

Storing Your Coffee Beans

Since coffee is a perishable food item, it is important to store your coffee beans properly before using them, if you want to make the best cup of coffee possible with the beans that you have.

In order to make the highest-quality cup of coffee, it is best to store your beans whole and grind them at home as you need them (see the section on grinding coffee, page 16).

Beans purchased in airtight (or vacuum-packed) bags will last for weeks or even months if unopened and stored at room temperature. Once the beans have been exposed to air, they should ideally be used within two weeks. Therefore, it is a good idea to buy your coffee on a regular basis, only as you need it.

When a bag of beans has been opened (or if the beans were purchased from an open bin at a specialty coffee shop), it should be stored in the freezer in an airtight container. They will remain fresh for a month or more. You can then take two weeks' worth of beans out of the freezer as you need them.

These beans should be stored in an airtight container at room temperature, or at about 60°F. (In warmer climates, they should be stored in the refrigerator.)

Ground coffee should be stored in an airtight container at room temperature (or in the refrigerator, depending on the climate), and for maximum freshness, it should be consumed within two weeks.

There are two basic types of coffee that we will be using in this book: brewed coffee and espresso.

Brewed coffee generally involves running hot water through coffee grounds, although it can be made using a cold-water process as well. Most brewed coffee is made with light- or medium-roast coffee, or with a dark roast like Viennese or French.

Espresso coffee describes not only the darkest roast of coffee bean (which is most often used for making espresso), but also the technique for making this type of coffee. Making espresso generally involves running hot water rapidly through finely ground espresso beans. This produces a small cup (or demitasse) of extremely strong-tasting coffee that usually needs to be sweetened with at least a little bit of sugar.

Tips for Making the Best Cup of Coffee

Here are a few tips for making the best cup of coffee possible with the equipment that you have:

1. Always use fresh water; your cup of coffee is only as good as the water that's used to make it.

2. In general, you should use 2 tablespoons of ground coffee for every 6 ounces of brewed coffee that you want to make. To make espresso, you generally use about 1 tablespoon of coffee for every $1\frac{1}{2}$ ounces of espresso.

3. Always use the proper grind for the equipment that you're using. Too fine a grind will cause overextraction, clogging of your filter, or small particles of coffee beans getting into your cup of coffee. Too coarse a grind will lead to underextraction and a weak, bitter cup of coffee as the water will go through the coffee too rapidly.

4. If you are using a manual device, use water that is just off the boil, so as not to "burn" the coffee.

5. Always serve your coffee immediately after you make it; never reheat your coffee or reuse your coffee grounds. (If you want to use your hot coffee later, pour it into a preheated thermos right after it's brewed.)

6. Be sure to clean your equipment regularly, so that coffee residues or mineral deposits don't build up that can ruin your future cups of coffee.

7. Never leave your coffee on the burner for more than 20 minutes. That will ruin it.

A Word About Filters

There are a number of different coffee filters available today, including those made with chlorine- or oxygen-bleached white paper, unbleached brown paper, or no paper at all (the so-called gold filter). The oxygen-bleached white filters are becoming increasingly popular because they are "friendly" to the environment. Brown filters, while also environmentally friendly, tend to leave a faint papery taste in the coffee. Gold filters (actually made of gold-plated steel) are desirable because they don't need to be replaced and don't filter out the natural oils of the coffee bean, as do the paper filters.

Grinding Coffee the Right Way

As explained earlier, it's extremely important to grind your coffee in the appropriate fashion, depending on the method of brewing that you're using.

The coarsest grind is used for percolators, French presses, and for the cold-water method of making coffee. Medium grinds are used for flat-bottomed drip makers and stove-top espresso makers. Fine grinds are used for cone-shaped drip filters, and very fine grinds are generally used for espresso machines. An extremely fine or powdery grind is used for making Turkish coffee in a jezve (see page 18).

Methods for Brewing Coffee

The method or methods you choose for making your coffee are largely a matter of personal preference, based on the taste of the coffee that each method produces, the ease of use of each technique, and even certain esthetic principles such as wanting to use a more traditional method rather than a modern one.

The most popular way of making coffee today is the *drip method*—either with a manual device by heating the water separately, or by using an electric machine. With the drip method, hot water is poured over the coffee grounds, which are placed in a filter above the carafe. This method offers convenience and a high-quality cup of coffee.

The *French press* (or plunger pot) method involves placing the coffee grounds at the bottom of a glass cylinder, pouring hot water over the grounds, letting them steep for 2 to 4 minutes, and then plunging a steel-mesh filter down to the bottom of the cylinder. This traps the grounds on the bottom and leaves the brewed coffee on top. Then you simply pour the coffee out of the carafe. The benefits of this method are that no paper filters are necessary and all of the coffee beans' essential oils remain in your cup of coffee—which is a rich one.

The *vacuum method* of making coffee consists of two glass pots that are placed one on top of the other and are connected by a glass tube with a filter. Water is placed in the bottom pot and coffee grounds in the top, and when the water is heated, it rises through the tube and spills over the grounds. When the pot is taken off of the heat source (be it a stove or a tabletop heat source), the brewed coffee falls back through the tube into the lower pot. This technique produces an extremely rich cup of coffee similar to that made with the French press method. However, it is much less commonly used.

Other methods for brewing coffee include using a *jezve,* the Neapolitan *flip-drip,* and the *percolator.*

The jezve is a long-handled brass or copper pot in which a small amount of water, coffee grounds, and usually sugar are placed, brought to a frothy boil, and then served in a demitasse cup. Often the froth is spooned into the cup twice before the coffee is poured out. This traditional (indeed, ancient) technique produces a rich, strong, almost muddy cup of coffee with plenty of grounds left on the bottom. You want to be careful to drink only the coffee, and not the grounds. (You can also make this type of coffee using a small saucepan.)

The Neapolitan flip-drip consists of two metal cylinders that are connected to each other, one on top of the other, with a filter in between. Water is placed in the bottom container and brought to a boil; then the entire device is turned upside down and the hot water drips down through ground coffee that has been placed in the filter. The now-bottom container has a spout through which the brewed coffee is poured. This technique produces a rich cup of coffee that tastes somewhat in between that produced by the gold filter and that produced by a stove-top espresso maker.

The percolator has become increasingly less popular in recent years, especially among gourmet coffee aficionados. This is because percolators not only boil the coffee but pass the heated water through the coffee grounds again and again. Because of this, the coffee's essential aroma and taste are basically burned out of it. The result is an often bitter cup of coffee.

One more method of brewing coffee should be discussed here: the *cold-water method.* With this process, cold water is added to very coarsely ground coffee in a large container and is allowed to steep for 10 to 24 hours, depending on how strong you want your coffee to be. Then the coffee is filtered into a carafe. It can be stored in the refrigerator for up to 3 weeks, this type of coffee can be drunk hot by using about $\frac{1}{3}$ cup of concentrate in every cup of hot water, or you can use it in iced coffee as you would extrastrength chilled coffee made with any hot-water process (see the following on making iced coffee). The result is a smooth, mild cup of coffee which is very low in acidity, as the cold-water process does not extract the oils of the coffee bean as thoroughly as does the hot-water process.

In order to make iced coffee using a standard hot-water brewing method, simply use $1\frac{1}{2}$ to 2 times the normal amount of coffee, brew it as you normally would, and pour it over ice—either immediately or after the coffee has cooled down to room temperature. It is best to use coffee made with this technique within 1 or 2 hours—no more than 3.

You can store this type of coffee in the refrigerator in a sealed container, but after about 1 day, the freshness and flavor of the coffee deteriorate dramatically. Therefore, it is always best to brew your iced coffee as soon as you can before drinking it. (You can also make coffee ice cubes with this mixture—or with cold-brewed coffee—that will not dilute your cup of iced coffee as will regular ice cubes.)

Making Espresso

There are basically two ways to make espresso: with a stove-top espresso maker or with an electric machine.

The stove-top espresso maker operates by heating water in the bottom chamber until it is forced up through the filter, which contains grounds of espresso roast coffee. Once the espresso reaches the top chamber, it can easily be poured out through the spout. A good steel stove-top espresso maker will make a quality demitasse of espresso in just a few minutes.

Some stove-top espresso makers also include a valve that can be used for steaming milk for cappuccinos. If you don't have one of these models, you can use an electric device that steams milk by heating water in a chamber and forcing it through a valve by steam pressure. (There is also a special stove-top device that you can use just for steaming milk.)

There are a number of electric espresso machines available today, and most of the less expensive ones are pretty comparable in terms of quality. The advantage here is that electric espresso machines also include a valve for steaming milk.

Cappuccino purists, however, may not be satisfied with the steaming capability of these less expensive machines, and may wish to purchase a more powerful espresso machine that approaches the commercial machines in terms of quality but is still affordable for the home user.

By contacting the manufacturers that are listed in the directory at the end of the book, you should be able to find just the right espresso machine for your purposes—and your budget.

Steaming Milk Properly

Perhaps a few words should be said here about how to steam milk properly with your home espresso machine for your cappuccinos and lattes.

In the first place, always start off with a cold pitcher (you can place it in the refrigerator beforehand). A stainless steel pitcher works best. Nonfat and low-fat milk are most widely used—although regular milk can be easily steamed once you get the hang of it.

Just fill the pitcher about one-third to one-half with the milk (no more than half, because the milk will expand when steamed). Place the nozzle of the steamer on the surface of the milk and turn the steam pressure all the way on.

As the steamer begins to froth the milk, lower the pitcher while the milk expands, keeping the nozzle about $\frac{1}{2}$ inch under the surface of the milk. Be careful not to let the milk boil, as it may overflow or have a bit of a burnt taste.

When the foam that you've produced by steaming the milk begins to rise to the surface of the pitcher, you can turn the pressure down or take the pitcher away from the steamer, as the milk is now just about to boil.

Ideally, steamed milk should contain very small bubbles throughout the liquid, and the foam on top should have a sweet or light taste to it. While steaming milk may seem rather awkward at first, with just a little bit of practice you'll really get the hang of it, and before long you should become an expert!

A Note on Ingredients

1. When not otherwise specified, regular granulated sugar (or other sweeteners, such as honey and brown sugar) can be added to any of these drinks, depending on your taste. Many of the drinks taste fine without any sugar at all. It's up to you.

2. It's always best to use fresh whipped cream—generally about $\frac{1}{4}$ cup per drink. Unless otherwise specified, whipped cream does not need to be sweetened, as you can sweeten the drink itself. However, if you wish to add a small amount of sugar to your whipped cream, there's no reason not to do so.

3. Low-fat or even nonfat milk can be substituted for whole milk, depending on your taste.

4. I use chocolate syrup in these recipes, but an equal amount of sweetened chocolate powder can be used as well. I also use sweetened chocolate powder as a topping, but if you're willing to make the effort, shaved or grated chocolate provides a more natural flavor. (Hint: Shave your chocolate slices beforehand and keep them in a sealed container in the refrigerator.)

5. I often use flavor extracts in these recipes, since these are the most readily available. Some specialty coffee shops carry flavored (and usually sweetened) syrups (or drops) that you can use in your gourmet coffee drinks. In general, 1 tablespoon of these flavored syrups (or a few drops) is the equivalent of $\frac{1}{4}$ teaspoon extract.

6. In the soda recipes, club soda can be substituted for carbonated (or sparkling) water.

7. If you wish to make more (or fewer) servings of these drinks, simply multiply (or divide) the amount of each ingredient to provide for the number of servings that you wish to make.

Once you understand the basics of good coffee making, it's time to start making drinks. This is simply a matter of mixing some of history's best flavors and spices with whatever type of coffee you like best at any given time of the day—or year, for that matter.

Perhaps you want a nice cappuccino in the morning, a delicious espresso after dinner, a tasty iced Caffè Latte (see page 42) on a hot summer afternoon, or a large mug of Viennese Coffee (see page 28) in front of the fireplace on a winter evening.

Throw in a little whipped cream, ice cream, carbonated water, or a slice of lemon or lime, depending on the drink you're making, and the combinations are virtually endless. You can even blend fresh fruit such as bananas, strawberries, and raspberries into your coffee drinks.

So why not get out your coffee maker and start making your own espressos, cappuccinos, lattes, mochas, and other gourmet coffee drinks in the comfort of your home. Just follow the recipes in these pages and you should be able to create a delicious gourmet coffee drink for just about any occasion.

Good luck! And, most of all, simply enjoy the results of your coffee-making efforts!

Hot

Drinks

Made

with

Brewed

Coffee

Unless otherwise specified, all of the drinks in this chapter are made with freshly brewed coffee that is still hot, and should be served immediately.

Café au Lait

This drink, popular throughout the world, enriches the standard cup of coffee with the delicate taste of steamed milk. You may wish to vary the proportions of coffee and milk, depending on your taste: for example, three-fourths coffee and one-fourth milk, or half coffee and half milk.

⅔ cup coffee
⅓ cup milk

Ground cinnamon or nutmeg, or sweetened chocolate powder (optional)

Pour the coffee into a cup. Steam the milk and add to the coffee, leaving a layer of foam on top. Sprinkle cinnamon, nutmeg, or chocolate powder on top of the foam, if desired.

Serves 1

Variation: For a Café Vermont, stir 3 tablespoons maple syrup into the coffee before adding the steamed milk. Proceed as directed above.

Café Mocha

This particular drink adds the taste of chocolate to a Café au Lait. As with the Café au Lait, the proportions of coffee and milk may be varied according to your taste.

⅔ cup coffee

2 tablespoons chocolate syrup

⅓ cup milk

Sweetened chocolate powder (optional)

Pour the coffee into a cup. Stir the chocolate syrup into the coffee. Steam the milk until hot and frothy, then add to the coffee, leaving a layer of foam on top. Sprinkle chocolate powder on top, if desired.

Serves 1

Variations: For a Café Mocha Mint, stir ⅛ teaspoon mint extract into the coffee along with the chocolate syrup. Proceed as directed above and garnish with a fresh mint sprig, if desired.

For a Mandarin Mocha, stir ⅛ teaspoon orange extract into the coffee along with the chocolate syrup. Proceed as directed above.

Viennese Coffee

A venerable tradition in Vienna's coffeehouses, this coffee's tasty flavor comes from the whipped cream topping.

2 cups coffee, preferably Viennese or other dark roast

½ cup heavy cream, whipped Ground cinnamon, nutmeg, or cloves

Pour the coffee into 2 cups. Top each cup with a large dollop of whipped cream and sprinkle with cinnamon, nutmeg, or cloves.

Serves 2

Café Borgia

The citrus taste adds zest to this drink, while beautifully complementing the whipped cream at the same time.

2 cups coffee
½ cup heavy cream, whipped

Grated orange peel

Divide the coffee into 2 cups. Top each cup with a large dollop of whipped cream and sprinkle with grated orange peel.

Serves 2

Café Belgique

This drink has an enjoyable light vanilla taste, which is a result of the egg white mixture that rises to the surface of the cup.

1 egg white	*¼ teaspoon vanilla extract*
½ cup heavy cream	*3 cups coffee*

Beat the egg white until stiff. Whip the cream along with the vanilla. Mix the egg white and whipped cream mixture together and fill 4 cups one-third of the way. Add ⅔ cup coffee to each cup.

Serves 4

Chocolate Cream Coffee

Serve this drink in front of a fire on a cold winter evening.

¼ cup heavy cream	*Ground cinnamon*
3 tablespoons chocolate syrup	*Sweetened chocolate powder*
1 cup coffee	*Grated orange peel*

Whip all but 1 tablespoon of the cream. Stir the reserved tablespoon of cream and the chocolate syrup in a saucepan over low heat until mixed together. Add the coffee gradually, stirring the mixture as you do so. Pour into a mug and top with whipped cream and cinnamon, chocolate powder, and grated orange peel.

Serves 1

Spiced Cream Coffee

The spicy whipped cream is delicious, and combines with the chocolate-flavored coffee to create a great taste.

> ¾ teaspoon ground
> cinnamon
>
> ¼ teaspoon ground
> nutmeg
>
> 1 tablespoon sugar

> ½ cup heavy cream
>
> 1½ cups coffee
>
> 2 teaspoons chocolate
> syrup

Stir ¼ teaspoon of the cinnamon and the nutmeg and sugar into the cream and whip. Divide the coffee into two 6-ounce portions and stir 1 teaspoon chocolate syrup and ¼ teaspoon cinnamon into each cup. Top with spiced whipped cream.

Serves 2

Spiced Coffee

Combining spices and coffee has been a tradition for as long as coffee has been consumed. You may want to experiment with your own combination—and amount—of spices.

> 1½ cups coffee
>
> 1 cinnamon stick
>
> 2 whole cloves
>
> ¼ teaspoon whole allspice

> ½ cup heavy cream,
> whipped
>
> Ground cinnamon
>
> White or brown sugar,
> to taste

Pour the coffee over the cinnamon stick, cloves, and allspice in a saucepan and simmer over low heat for 5 to 7 minutes. Strain into cups, top with whipped cream, and sprinkle with cinnamon. Add white or brown sugar to taste.

Serves 2

Variation: Omit the cinnamon stick and allspice and substitute 2 strips each of orange and lemon peel; use 10 cloves instead of 2. Proceed as directed above.

Café Vanilla

This drink is fun to make, and the natural flavor of the vanilla bean is a nice reward that you can taste with each sip. If you use an espresso or other dark roast when you brew your coffee, you can approximate the taste of a cappuccino with this drink.

¼ *vanilla bean*   ¾ *cup coffee*
½ *cup milk*   *Ground cinnamon or*
1 *teaspoon brown sugar*   *nutmeg*

Slice the vanilla bean lengthwise and place it with the milk and brown sugar in a saucepan. Bring to a boil, stirring occasionally. Remove from the heat, cover, and let stand for a few minutes. Take out the vanilla bean and blend the milk mixture in a blender for about 30 seconds, or until it becomes frothy. Add to the hot coffee and top with cinnamon or nutmeg.

Serves 1

Cinnamon-Vanilla Coffee

Here the taste of cinnamon is added to that of vanilla to make for a delightful taste combination. The brown sugar–whipped cream topping gives it a little extra pizzazz!

$1\frac{1}{2}$ cups coffee

$\frac{1}{4}$ vanilla bean, sliced

1 cinnamon stick

$\frac{1}{2}$ cup heavy cream

1 tablespoon or more brown sugar

Before brewing the coffee, slice the vanilla bean lengthwise and place it with the cinnamon stick in the bottom of the coffee maker carafe. While the coffee is brewing, whip the cream and brown sugar together. Pour the coffee into 2 cups and top with the whipped cream mixture. Add extra brown sugar to taste, if desired.

Serves 2

Chocolate-Vanilla Coffee

Chocolate and vanilla are a natural taste combination—each complements the other. You can pour over ice for a cool taste, too!

1 tablespoon chocolate syrup

$\frac{1}{4}$ teaspoon vanilla extract

1 cup coffee

$\frac{1}{4}$ cup heavy cream, whipped

Stir the chocolate syrup and vanilla into the hot coffee. Top with whipped cream.

Serves 1

Coffee Grog

The addition of brown sugar and butter makes this spicy drink even richer, while orange and lemon peel give it just the extra flavor it needs.

2 tablespoons butter

1 cup brown sugar

⅛ teaspoon ground allspice

⅛ teaspoon ground cinnamon

⅛ teaspoon ground nutmeg

⅛ teaspoon ground cloves

1½ cups heavy cream or half-and-half

12 small strips of orange peel

12 small strips of lemon peel

9 cups coffee

1½ teaspoons rum extract (optional)

Melt the butter in a saucepan over low heat. Stir in the brown sugar, allspice, cinnamon, nutmeg, and cloves, and allow the mixture to cool. Store in a sealed container in the refrigerator.

To serve, combine in each cup 1 teaspoon of the butter mixture, 2 tablespoons cream, 1 strip orange peel, and 1 strip lemon peel. Add 6 ounces of hot coffee and stir. You can also add ⅛ teaspoon rum extract to each cup of grog, if desired.

Serves 12

Variation: Omit the allspice and cinnamon and double the amount of ground nutmeg and cloves. Proceed as directed above.

Turkish Coffee

The fun of making Turkish coffee lies in the use of the jezve (see page 18). Conjuring up images of the ancient Middle East as you make your coffee will prepare you for the strong taste of the coffee as you sip it. (Be careful not to drink the grounds!) This method of making coffee is common throughout the Middle East, and should more accurately be called Middle Eastern coffee. Some of the best beans to use are Mocha, Java, and Viennese roast.

1 tablespoon extremely fine ground or powdered coffee

½ to 2 teaspoons sugar (optional)

2 ounces cold water

In a jezve, stir all the ingredients together. Place over low heat and slowly bring this mixture to a boil (do not stir). When it reaches the boiling point, remove from the heat and pour into a demitasse. Let the grounds settle before drinking, or add a tiny splash of cold water to help settle the grounds.

Serves 1

Variations: For a frothier drink, let the coffee foam up, remove the pot from the heat, and spoon the top froth into your cup. Return the pot to the fire and repeat twice more, then pour the liquid into the cup. For interesting taste sensations, add ⅛ teaspoon ground cardamom, cinnamon, nutmeg, or cloves to the ground coffee before brewing. For a rich, creamy drink, use milk instead of water.

Hawaiian Coffee

Try this tropical drink on a warm summer evening, or use it to warm yourself up on a cold winter day.

½ cup milk   ½ cup coffee
½ cup sweetened shredded
   coconut

Preheat the oven to 350°F. Place the milk and coconut in a saucepan and warm over low heat for 2 to 3 minutes, stirring occasionally. Strain the milk and place the coconut on a baking sheet in the oven until it turns brown, about 8 to 10 minutes. Add the milk to the hot coffee and top with the browned coconut.

Serves 1

New Orleans Coffee

The secret of this coffee is the earthy taste of the chicory. Use a dark roast of coffee, and mix the chicory into the ground coffee before brewing as usual. You may want to vary the proportions of coffee and milk, for example using two-thirds coffee and one-third milk, or one-third coffee and two-thirds milk. The amount of chicory can also vary, from 20 to 40 percent, depending on your taste.

1 cup coffee, with 25 percent ground chicory	*1 cup steamed milk*
	Ground cinnamon

Pour the coffee into two cups. Add steamed milk evenly to both and top off each cup with some froth from the steamed milk. Sprinkle cinnamon on top.

Serves 2

Spiced Coffee Cider

On a crisp autumn afternoon, have some fun making this coffee, and then sit back and enjoy its taste.

½ cup coffee	*⅛ teaspoon ground cloves*
½ cup apple juice	*⅛ teaspoon ground allspice*
1 cinnamon stick	*1 teaspoon brown sugar*
1 thin slice of orange, including rind	*Ground cinnamon (optional)*

Stir all the ingredients except cinnamon together in a saucepan and simmer over low heat for 3 to 4 minutes, stirring occasionally. Strain into a mug and sprinkle with cinnamon, if desired.

Serves 1

Blended Banana Coffee

Drink this concoction as soon as you can after making it—before it has time to settle.

1 tablespoon butter

½ banana, peeled, sliced, and mashed

½ teaspoon ground cinnamon

¼ teaspoon vanilla extract

1 cup hot coffee

½ cup heavy cream

1 tablespoon confectioners' sugar

Melt the butter in a saucepan over low heat. Stir in the banana, cinnamon, and vanilla. Simmer for 1 to 2 minutes, stirring occasionally. Remove from the heat. Place the coffee, cream, and sugar in the blender and add the banana mixture. Blend for 15 to 20 seconds, or until smooth. Serve at once.

Serves 1

Hot
Drinks
Made
with
Espresso

All of the drinks in this section begin with a basic espresso drink. From this starting point, the combinations are virtually endless. The following drinks represent the most popular among those that are served in today's gourmet coffee shops—and include many traditional favorites as well. *Experiment all you want with the amount and strength of the espresso that you use in each drink, as well as with any of the other ingredients—milk, flavors, and spices.* The rewards will be there for you with every sip. *Enjoy!*

E s p r e s s o : An espresso consists of about 1½ ounces of extremely strong-tasting coffee. It is made with a dark-roasted bean, using either a stove-top espresso maker or an electric machine. It serves as the basis for many gourmet coffee drinks, both hot and cold, and has numerous variations of its own. Add almond, rum, brandy, mint, or vanilla extract to taste, if desired. You can also sprinkle spices such as ground cinnamon and cardamom onto your espresso.

D o u b l e E s p r e s s o : Use twice the amount of water and coffee grounds as you would for a single espresso.

R i s t r e t t o : Use the same amount of grounds as for a single espresso, but stop the flow of water at about 1 ounce. This is also known as a "short" espresso.

Espresso Romano: A single espresso served with a small slice of lemon peel.

Espresso Anise: A single espresso with $\frac{1}{8}$ teaspoon anise extract added. For an Espresso Anise Royale, top with whipped cream.

Americano: A single espresso with hot water added to taste (usually about 1 cup).

Red Eye: A single espresso added to 1 cup brewed coffee.

Macchiato: A single espresso with a dollop of foam from steamed milk (1 to 2 tablespoons) on top.

Espresso con Panna: A single espresso topped with whipped cream.

Espresso Borgia: A single espresso topped with whipped cream (or froth from steamed milk) and grated orange peel.

Espresso Grog: Prepare a grog mixture as described in the recipe for Coffee Grog (see page 33). For each cup of Espresso Grog, place 1 teaspoon of the grog mixture in the bottom of the cup, along with 1 tablespoon heavy cream (or half-and-half), 1 small strip orange peel, and 1 small strip lemon peel. Add a single espresso to each of these cups and stir in the grog mixture thoroughly. You can also add a tiny amount (less than $\frac{1}{8}$ teaspoon) of rum extract to each cup of grog, if desired.

Makes 12 servings

Cappuccino: This drink consists of one-third espresso (a single) and one-third steamed milk, and is topped with one-third foam from the steamed milk. Sprinkle ground cinnamon, nutmeg, or sweetened chocolate powder on top, if desired. You can also add almond, rum, brandy, mint, or vanilla extract to taste. For a Double Cappuccino, use a double espresso instead of a single.

Cappuccino Royale: A cappuccino topped with whipped cream, and often with almond, rum, brandy, mint, or vanilla extract added to taste. Garnish with a thin wafer.

Butterscotch Cappuccino: Add butterscotch syrup to a cappuccino to taste. For a Butterscotch Latte, do the same thing with a Caffè Latte.

Caffè Latte: This drink consists of a single espresso with the rest of the glass filled up with steamed milk, and is topped off with a thin layer of foam from the steamed milk. Sprinkle ground cinnamon, nutmeg, or sweetened chocolate powder on top, if desired. You can also add almond, rum, brandy, mint, or vanilla extract to taste. For a Double Caffè Latte, use a double espresso instead of a single.

Latte Macchiato: Put steamed milk, topped with foam from the steamed milk into a glass; then gently pour a single espresso into the glass. The espresso will slowly drip to the bottom.

Mochaccino: This drink consists of one-third espresso (a single), one-third steamed chocolate milk, and one-third foam from the steamed chocolate milk for topping. (You can also make this drink by stirring chocolate syrup into the espresso, adding one-third steamed milk, and topping it off with one-third foam from the steamed milk.) Top with whipped cream and sweetened chocolate powder, if desired. For a Double Mochaccino, use a double espresso instead of a single.

Mocha Latte: This drink consists of a single espresso with the rest of the glass filled up with steamed chocolate milk, and topped off with a thin layer of foam from the steamed chocolate milk. (You can also make this drink by stirring chocolate syrup into the espresso, filling up the rest of the glass with steamed milk, and topping it off with a thin layer of foam from the steamed milk.) Top with whipped cream and sweetened chocolate powder, if desired. For a Double Mocha Latte, use a double espresso instead of a single.

Spiced Chocolate Espresso

The taste of espresso comes alive in this spicy drink.

> 2 double espressos
> (page 40)
> 2 ounces heavy cream or
> half-and-half
> ¼ teaspoon ground
> cinnamon
>
> ⅛ teaspoon ground nutmeg
> 2 teaspoons sugar
> 2 teaspoons chocolate syrup
> Whipped cream

Mix all the ingredients except the chocolate syrup and whipped cream in a pitcher and steam until hot and frothy. Pour into 2 mugs, add 1 teaspoon chocolate syrup to each, and stir. Top with whipped cream.

Serves 2

Cold

Drinks

Made

with

Brewed

Coffee

U*nless otherwise specified, all of the drinks in this section are made with cold coffee. In order to account for the dilution factor of ice cubes, you should brew coffee using one-and-a-half times to twice the amount of ground coffee per cup than normal. Then store the coffee in a sealed container in the refrigerator.*

Iced Mint Coffee

Enjoy the minty taste of this cool drink on a warm summer evening.

½ cup coffee
⅛ teaspoon mint extract
1 tablespoon heavy cream,
*   or ¼ cup milk or*
*   half-and-half*

Ice cubes
Fresh mint sprig, for
garnish

Mix together the coffee, mint, and cream. Pour over ice. Garnish with a fresh mint sprig.

Serves 1

Variations: Omit the cream and proceed as directed above, or omit the mint extract and mint sprig and substitute ⅛ teaspoon almond, rum, brandy, or vanilla extract.

Iced Café au Lait

The foam on top of this drink provides a delicate taste through which to drink your coffee.

Ice cubes

$\frac{1}{3}$ cup milk

$\frac{2}{3}$ cup coffee

Fill a glass with ice. Pour in the coffee. Steam the milk and pour into the glass, leaving a layer of foam on top.

Serves 1

Iced Almond Coffee

Here's a sweet drink with a little treat to top it off!

4 cups coffee

2 cups half-and-half

4 tablespoons sweetened
 condensed milk

2 tablespoons sugar

1 teaspoon almond extract

Ice cubes

1 cup heavy cream, whipped
 Sliced almonds, for
 garnish

Mix the coffee, half-and-half, condensed milk, sugar, and almond in a pitcher. Pour over ice in 4 glasses or mugs. Top each portion with whipped cream and garnish with a few slices of almond.

Serves 4

Spiced Iced Coffee I

The combination of spices and coffee works just as well in cold drinks as in hot ones. This and the following recipes should give you some ideas for spice mixtures. You may also want to experiment on your own, depending on which spices you like best.

1½ cups freshly brewed
coffee
1½ tablespoons sugar
1 cinnamon stick
3 whole cloves

⅛ teaspoon ground allspice
Ice cubes
Whipped cream
(optional)

Place all the ingredients except the ice and whipped cream in a saucepan and warm over low heat. Stir until the sugar is dissolved. Let the mixture cool to room temperature, about 30 minutes. Remove the cinnamon stick and cloves, and pour over ice. Top with whipped cream, if desired.

Serves 2

Spiced Iced Coffee II

Here is another, slightly different method of making spiced coffee ahead of time, to serve whenever you wish.

2 cinnamon sticks	*4 cups freshly brewed coffee*
4 whole cloves	*Ice cubes*
¼ teaspoon whole allspice	*Milk (optional)*
¼ teaspoon cardamom seeds	*Brown sugar (optional)*

Place the cinnamon sticks, cloves, allspice, and cardamom seeds at the bottom of a container, and pour coffee over the spices. Let the mixture cool to room temperature, about 30 minutes. Strain into a new container and store in the refrigerator.

When ready to serve, pour over ice and add milk and brown sugar, if desired.

Serves 4 to 6

V a r i a t i o n : Omit the four spices and add 4 strips each of orange and lemon peel, and 8 cloves. Proceed as directed above.

Iced Cardamom Coffee

Cardamom works just as well with cold coffee as with hot. You can pretend you're in a Middle Eastern bazaar while you drink this one.

½ teaspoon cardamom seeds

2 cups water

4 tablespoons coffee grounds

Ice cubes

Sugar, to taste

Lemon or pineapple slices, or maraschino cherries, for garnish

Boil the cardamom seeds in the water for about 5 minutes. Strain and use this water to brew your coffee. Pour the coffee over ice and sweeten with sugar to taste. Garnish with slices of lemon or pineapple or with maraschino cherries.

Serves 2

Honey Iced Coffee

This is a smooth, sweet drink. If you stir the honey in first, you'll avoid having it harden after the ice is added.

Honey, to taste

1 cup freshly brewed coffee

Ice cubes

Whipped cream (optional)

Ground cinnamon and nutmeg

Stir the honey into the coffee to taste. Add ice and top with whipped cream, if desired. Sprinkle with cinnamon and nutmeg.

Serves 1

Iced Maple Coffee

On a hot day, try this drink for a great taste of Vermont.

3 tablespoons maple syrup

1 cup freshly brewed
  coffee

Ice cubes

¼ cup heavy cream,
  whipped

Stir the maple syrup into the coffee and pour over ice. Top with whipped cream.

Serves 1

Iced Coffee Bitters

Bitters add a tangy taste to this cooling drink.

½ teaspoon bitters

1 teaspoon vanilla extract

4 tablespoons sugar

4½ cups coffee

Ice cubes

Whipped cream or half-
  and-half (optional)

Mix the bitters, vanilla, and sugar together with 2 tablespoons of the coffee until the mixture is a thick syrup. Add 2½ teaspoons of this mixture to every 6 ounces of coffee. Serve over ice. Top with whipped cream or lightly pour 2 tablespoons half-and-half onto the top of each drink, if desired.

Serves 6

Coffee Soda

Adding carbonated water to coffee provides a nice sparkle for your drinks. The fruit garnish supplies a little punch as well.

½ cup coffee
Ice cubes
¼ cup carbonated water (or cola)

Strip of lemon, orange, or lime peel, for garnish

Pour the coffee over ice. Add carbonated water and garnish with a small strip of lemon, orange, or lime peel.

Serves 1

Coffee Ice Cream Soda

The addition of ice cream creates a frosty, old-fashioned treat.

½ cup coffee
1 ounce half-and-half (optional)
Ice cubes

¼ cup carbonated water (or cola)
1 scoop vanilla ice cream

Pour the coffee and half-and-half, if desired, over ice in a tall glass. Add the carbonated water and ice cream.

Serves 1

Variations: Substitute 1 scoop of chocolate or coffee ice cream for the vanilla. Proceed as directed above.

Rum Coffee Soda

With the taste of rum, you can pretend you're in the Caribbean.

1 cup coffee
¼ cup half-and-half
¼ teaspoon rum extract

Ice cubes
½ cup carbonated water
Sugar, to taste

Mix the coffee, half-and-half, and rum together and pour over ice in two tall glasses. Add carbonated water and sugar to taste.

Serves 2

Chocolate Coffee Float

This is another time-honored drink that actually tastes as good as it sounds.

2 scoops chocolate
    ice cream
1 cup coffee

¼ cup heavy cream, whipped
Sweetened chocolate
    powder

Add the ice cream to the coffee in a tall glass. Top with whipped cream and chocolate powder.

Serves 1

Variations: Substitute 2 scoops of vanilla or coffee ice cream for the chocolate. Proceed as directed above.

Hot Coffee Float

Hot coffee is the secret to the success of this drink. As the ice cream melts, all of the tastes blend together.

1 scoop each vanilla, chocolate, and coffee ice cream

¾ cup freshly brewed coffee, still piping hot

¼ cup heavy cream, whipped

Place the scoops of ice cream in a tall glass and add the coffee. Top with the whipped cream.

Serves 1

Blended Vanilla Coffee

A light, fluffy drink, this has a smooth vanilla taste.

½ cup coffee

1 cup milk

½ teaspoon vanilla extract

1 tablespoon sugar

Ice cubes

Ground cinnamon (optional)

Mix all the ingredients except the ice and cinnamon in a blender for 15 to 20 seconds, or until frothy. Pour over ice in a tall glass, and top with a dash of cinnamon, if desired.

Serves 1

Blended Chocolate Coffee

Here's another light, fluffy drink, this time with a smooth, chocolaty taste.

½ cup coffee	Ice cubes
2 cups milk	Whipped cream (optional)
2 tablespoons chocolate syrup	Sweetened chocolate powder (optional)
1 tablespoon sugar	

Mix the coffee, milk, chocolate syrup, and sugar in a blender for 15 to 20 seconds, or until frothy. Pour over ice in 2 tall glasses and top with whipped cream and chocolate powder, if desired.

Serves 2

Blended Honey Coffee

For an easy but good cup of coffee first thing in the morning, try this one.

¾ cup coffee	1 tablespoon honey
¾ cup milk	

Mix all the ingredients together in a blender for 10 to 15 seconds.

Serves 1

Banana Coffee Blend

Serve this drink right away, before it has time to settle.

1 cup coffee
1 cup milk
1 banana, peeled and sliced

1 tablespoon confectioners'
sugar

Mix all the ingredients together in a blender for 15 to 20 seconds, or until smooth.

Serves 1

Coffee Crush

This is best consumed immediately.

$\frac{3}{4}$ cup coffee
1$\frac{1}{4}$ cups crushed ice
Sugar to taste
Ice cubes
Whipped cream
(optional)

Sweetened chocolate
powder, ground
cinnamon or nutmeg
(optional)

Mix the coffee, crushed ice, and sugar in a blender for 15 to 20 seconds, or until frothy. Pour over ice, top with whipped cream, and sprinkle with chocolate powder, cinnamon, or nutmeg, if desired.

Serves 2

Chocolate-Coffee Crush

A favorite in most of today's gourmet coffee shops, this tastes like a chocolate-coffee milkshake.

¾ cup coffee

½ cup milk

½ cup crushed ice

2 tablespoons
chocolate syrup

Sugar, to taste

Whipped cream (optional)

Sweetened chocolate
powder (optional)

Mix all the ingredients except the whipped cream and chocolate powder in a blender for 15 to 20 seconds, or until smooth. Pour into a tall glass and top with whipped cream and chocolate powder, if desired.

Serves 1

Variations: For a Vanilla-Coffee Crush, omit the chocolate syrup and substitute ¼ teaspoon vanilla extract. Proceed as directed above.

For a Creamy Coffee Crush, simply omit the chocolate syrup.

Vanilla-Chocolate Coffee Shake

The hint of cinnamon makes this a delicious drink.

½ cup coffee
1 tablespoon chocolate
  syrup
2 scoops vanilla ice cream

⅛ teaspoon ground
  cinnamon
Whipped cream
  (optional)

Mix all the ingredients except the whipped cream in a blender for 15 to 20 seconds, or until smooth. Top with whipped cream, if desired.

Serves 1

58

Variations: For a Chocolate Coffee Shake, omit the vanilla ice cream and cinnamon and substitute 2 scoops of chocolate ice cream and ⅛ teaspoon ground nutmeg. Proceed as directed above.

    For a Coffee Coffee Shake, substitute 2 scoops of coffee ice cream for the vanilla ice cream and cinnamon.

Vanilla-Banana Coffee Shake

You will savor every sip of this creamy, rich shake.

½ cup coffee
½ banana, peeled and sliced
2 scoops vanilla ice cream
⅛ teaspoon almond extract

⅛ teaspoon ground
  cinnamon
Whipped cream
  (optional)

Mix all the ingredients except the whipped cream in a blender for 15 to 20 seconds, or until smooth. Top with whipped cream, if desired.

Serves 1

Vanilla-Rum Coffee Shake

The rum gives this drink a delightful flavor.

1½ cups coffee
2 scoops vanilla ice cream

½ teaspoon rum extract
Ice cubes

Mix all the ingredients except the ice in a blender for 15 to 20 seconds, or until smooth. Pour over ice in tall glasses.

Serves 2

Yogurt Coffee Shake

This drink is a perfect treat at lunch.

½ cup coffee
1 cup vanilla yogurt
¼ teaspoon vanilla extract

1 teaspoon confectioners' sugar

Mix all the ingredients together in a blender for 15 to 20 seconds, or until smooth.

Serves 1

Butterscotch Coffee Shake

For butterscotch lovers, this drink is a natural.

5 ounces coffee

2¼ tablespoons heavy cream

1 scoop vanilla (or coffee)
  ice cream

2 tablespoons butterscotch
  syrup

Mix all the ingredients together in a blender for 15 to 20 seconds,
or until smooth.

Serves 1

Tropical Coffee Delight

You will enjoy sipping this drink slowly on a hot summer day.

½ cup coffee

¼ cup papaya nectar

½ kiwi fruit, peeled and
  sliced

1 tablespoon cream of
  coconut

1 scoop vanilla ice cream

3–4 tablespoons heavy cream
  (optional)

Mix the coffee, papaya, ¼ kiwi, coconut, and ice cream in a blender
for 15 to 20 seconds, or until smooth. Garnish with the remaining kiwi and pour the heavy cream lightly on top, if desired.

Serves 1

Strawberry Delight

The combination of coffee, cream, and strawberries (or other fresh fruit) makes this a very unique drink, in all of its variations.

½ cup heavy cream

½ cup coffee

4 strawberries

¼ teaspoon almond extract

Confectioners' sugar, to taste

Additional strawberries, for garnish

Ice cubes (optional)

Whip ¼ cup of the cream and set aside. Mix the coffee, remaining cream, 4 strawberries, almond, and sugar in a blender for 15 to 20 seconds, or until smooth. Top with the whipped cream and garnish with fresh strawberries. (You can also pour this drink over ice, if desired.)

Serves 1

Variations: For a Raspberry Delight, omit the strawberries and substitute 12 raspberries. Proceed as directed above. Garnish with fresh raspberries.

For a Kiwi Delight, substitute 1 kiwi fruit, peeled and sliced, for the strawberries. Proceed as directed above. Garnish with a few slices of kiwi.

Cold

Drinks

Made

with

Espresso

A*ll of the drinks in this section begin with a basic espresso drink. In most cases, you'll be able to use freshly made espresso, since the amount you'll be using for each drink will be small enough to allow it to cool quickly when poured over ice. If you let the espresso cool down for a few minutes after making it, less ice will melt and you'll end up with a cooler drink. You may want to make a large batch of espresso and store it in a sealed container in the refrigerator. However, as with brewed coffee, after about a day the freshness and flavor of the espresso will deteriorate dramatically. Therefore, when using espresso in cold drinks, it is best to make the espresso as late as you can before drinking it. Since cold drinks are usually consumed in larger quantities than are hot drinks, you may wish to use double espressos for many of these drinks. However, as with hot espresso drinks, you should experiment with the volume and strength of the espresso that you use, as well as with any of the other ingredients, such as milk, flavors, and spices. Here are some favorites as well as traditional coffees that are available in most gourmet coffee shops around the country. Salut!*

Iced Espresso: A single or double espresso poured over ice cubes. Garnish with a small slice of lemon peel, if desired.

Iced Americano: Add hot water to a single espresso to taste, then pour over ice cubes.

Iced Macchiato: An iced espresso with a dollop of foam from steamed milk (1 to 2 tablespoons) on top.

Iced Espresso con Panna: An iced espresso topped with whipped cream.

Iced Maple Espresso: Stir 2 tablespoons maple syrup into a single espresso. Pour over ice cubes and top with whipped cream, if desired. For a Double Iced Maple Espresso, use twice the amount of maple syrup and espresso as for a single.

Iced Cappuccino: This drink consists of one-third espresso (a single), one-third cold milk, and one-third foam topping from steamed milk, over ice cubes. Sprinkle ground cinnamon or nutmeg or sweetened chocolate powder on top, and garnish with a fresh mint leaf, if desired. You can also add almond, rum, brandy, mint, or vanilla extract to taste. For a Double Iced Cappuccino, use a double espresso instead of a single.

Iced Cappuccino Royale: An iced cappuccino topped with whipped cream and garnished with a thin wafer. Add almond, rum, brandy, mint, or vanilla extract to taste, if desired.

Iced Caffè Latte: Pour a single espresso over ice cubes in a tall glass. Fill the rest of glass with cold milk and top with a thin layer of foam from steamed milk. Sprinkle ground cinnamon or nutmeg or sweetened chocolate powder on top, and garnish with a mint leaf, if desired. You can also add almond, rum, brandy, mint, or vanilla extract to taste. For a Double Iced Caffè Latte, use a double espresso instead of a single.

Iced Mochaccino: This drink consists of one-third espresso (a single), one-third cold chocolate milk, and one-third foam topping from steamed chocolate (or regular) milk, over ice cubes. Top with whipped cream and sweetened chocolate powder, if desired. For a Double Iced Mochaccino, use a double espresso instead of a single.

Iced Mocha Latte: Pour a single espresso over ice cubes in a tall glass. Fill the rest of glass with cold chocolate milk. Add a thin layer of foam from steamed chocolate (or regular) milk and top with whipped cream and sweetened chocolate powder, if desired. For a Double Iced Mocha Latte, use a double espresso instead of a single.

Espresso Soda

This drink is refreshing and surprisingly strong.

Single espresso (page 40)
Ice cubes
½ cup carbonated water (or cola)

Lemon, orange, or lime peel, for garnish

Pour the espresso over ice. Add carbonated water and garnish with a small piece of lemon, orange, or lime peel.

Serves 1

Variation: For a Double Espresso Soda, use double the amount of espresso and carbonated water (or cola).

Rum Espresso Soda

The rum flavor gives this drink an exotic taste.

Single espresso (page 40)
¼ cup heavy cream
¼ teaspoon rum extract

Ice cubes
½ cup carbonated water
Sugar, to taste

Mix the espresso, cream, and rum together and pour over ice. Add the carbonated water and sugar to taste.

Serves 1

Blended Honey Latte
🫘🫘

This drink, you will find, is a great pick-me-up.

> *Single espresso (page 40)*   *1 teaspoon honey*
> *¾ cup milk*

Mix all the ingredients together in a blender for 10 to 15 seconds.

S e r v e s   1

Espresso Float
🫘 🫘

This is a perfect dessert—sweet, and filling.

> *Double espresso (page 40)*   *Sweetened chocolate*
> *¼ cup milk*   *powder*
> *2 scoops vanilla ice cream*   *1 cinnamon stick, for*
> *¼ cup heavy cream, whipped*   *garnish*

Pour the espresso into a tall glass. Add the milk and ice cream and top with whipped cream and chocolate powder. Garnish with the cinnamon stick.

S e r v e s   1

V a r i a t i o n s : Instead of vanilla ice cream, use 2 scoops of chocolate or coffee ice cream. Proceed as directed above.

For a Cappuccino Float, use a hot or iced cappuccino with 1 scoop of vanilla ice cream. For a Chocoloccino, use chocolate ice cream.

For a Mochaccino Float, use a hot or iced mochaccino with 1 scoop of vanilla ice cream.

Espresso Ice Cream Soda

This drink is sure to satisfy.

Single espresso (page 40)
1 ounce half-and-half
(optional)
Ice cubes

½ cup carbonated water (or cola)
1 scoop vanilla ice cream

Pour espresso and half-and-half, if desired, over ice. Add carbonated water and ice cream.

Serves 1

Espresso Crush

Whipped cream makes this drink much richer.

Double espresso
(page 40)
½ cup crushed ice
Sugar, to taste
Ice cubes

Whipped cream (optional)
Sweetened chocolate
powder, ground
cinnamon or nutmeg
(optional)

Mix the espresso, crushed ice, and sugar in a blender for 15 to 20 seconds, or until frothy. Pour over ice. If desired, top with whipped cream and sprinkle with chocolate powder, cinnamon, or nutmeg.

Serves 1

Chocolate Espresso Crush

You may wish to use two scoops of ice cream instead of crushed ice in this drink, which is like an espresso shake.

Double espresso
(page 40)
¼ cup milk
½ cup crushed ice
2 tablespoons chocolate
syrup

Sugar, to taste
Whipped cream (optional)
Sweetened chocolate
powder (optional)

Mix all the ingredients except the whipped cream and chocolate powder in a blender for 15 to 20 seconds, or until smooth. Top with whipped cream and chocolate powder, if desired.

Serves 1

Variations: For a Vanilla Espresso Crush, substitute ⅛ teaspoon vanilla extract for the chocolate syrup.

For a Creamy Espresso Crush, omit the chocolate syrup.

Tropical Espresso Delight

This sweet, tangy drink still has the taste of espresso coming through.

*Single espresso
(page 40)*

⅛ cup papaya nectar

*1 teaspoon cream of
coconut*

*¼ kiwi fruit, peeled and
sliced*

½ scoop vanilla ice cream

*1 to 2 tablespoons heavy cream
(optional)*

Mix the espresso, papaya, coconut, ⅛ kiwi, and the ice cream in a blender for 15 to 20 seconds, or until smooth. Garnish with the remaining kiwi and pour the cream lightly on top, if desired.

Serves 1

Gourmet *Coffee* **Drinks** *with* **Liquor**

Just as various flavors and spices can be added to your gourmet coffee drinks, so can a wide variety of liquors. The combinations are virtually endless, but among the most popular additions are rum, whiskey, and such liqueurs as brandy, cognac, crème de menthe, crème de cacao, amaretto, anisette, Irish cream, Kahlúa and Tia Maria, Cointreau and Grand Marnier, Galliano and Frangelico. Liquors such as these can be used in combination with each other—using either hot or cold brewed coffee or espresso—and they can also be added to a cup of coffee all by themselves. You may also wish to add a little bit of kirsch, vodka, tequila, gin, curaçao, crème de banana, cherry liqueur, calvados, Benedictine, Tuaca, Strega, Sambuca, or Drambuie to your coffee, depending on your taste. By all means experiment with the quantity and combination of liquors you use in each drink, as well as with the amount of coffee, milk, flavors, spices, and other ingredients that you wish to use. Who knows? You just might develop a few interesting concoctions of your own. The recipes in this chapter are for hot and cold potables made with regular brewed coffee or espresso. Enjoy!

Hot Drinks Made with Brewed Coffee

These drinks are made with freshly brewed coffee and should be served immediately.

Bailey's–Crème de Cacao Coffee

Whether you use Frangelico or amaretto, it will be a sweet, refreshing concoction that is sure to satisfy.

1½ tablespoons Bailey's
   Original Irish Cream
1½ tablespoons crème de
   cacao
¼ teaspoon Frangelico

¾ cup coffee
¼ cup heavy cream,
   whipped
Ground cinnamon

Combine the Bailey's, crème de cacao, and Frangelico in a glass and add the coffee. Top with whipped cream and a dash of cinnamon.

Serves 1

Variation: Substitute ¼ teaspoon amaretto for the Frangelico. Proceed as directed above.

Café Brûlot

This is a fun drink for a winter afternoon because the process of making it is as warming as drinking the concoction itself.

1½ ounces brandy or
  cognac
1 teaspoon white or brown
  sugar
2 whole cloves
1 cinnamon stick

1 strip orange peel
1 strip lemon peel
¾ cup coffee
1 teaspoon Cointreau or
  Grand Marnier
  (optional)

Place all the ingredients except the coffee and Cointreau in a saucepan and warm over low heat for 1 to 2 minutes, stirring occasionally. Add the coffee and stir into the mixture. Strain into a cup. Add the Cointreau, if desired.

Serves 1

Kahlúa–Crème de Menthe Coffee

The taste of the coffee liqueur comes through in this peppermint-flavored drink.

2 tablespoons Kahlúa
2 tablespoons crème de
  menthe
¾ cup coffee

¼ cup heavy cream, whipped
Sweetened chocolate
  powder

Mix the Kahlúa and crème de menthe in a glass. Add the coffee and top with whipped cream and chocolate powder.

Serves 1

Variation: For a Kahlúa–Crème de Cacao Coffee, omit the crème de menthe and substitute 2 tablespoons crème de cacao. Proceed as directed above.

Kahlúa–Grand Marnier Coffee

This orangy drink retains the creamy coffee taste of the Bailey's and the Kahlúa.

1½ teaspoons Kahlúa

1½ teaspoons Grand Marnier

1½ teaspoons Bailey's Original Irish Cream

1½ teaspoons Frangelico

¾ cup coffee

¼ cup heavy cream, whipped

Grated orange peel, for garnish

Combine the Kahlúa, Grand Marnier, Bailey's, and Frangelico in a glass. Add the coffee and top with whipped cream. Garnish with orange peel.

Serves 1

Irish Coffee

This is a classic drink, popular throughout the world—and for good reason!

1 teaspoon sugar
2 tablespoons Irish whiskey
⅔ cup coffee

¼ cup heavy cream, lightly whipped

Place the sugar and whiskey in glass, add the coffee, and stir. Top with lightly whipped cream.

Serves 1

Kioki Coffee

The blend of brandy and Kahlúa gives this drink a unique taste. The whipped cream makes it even more special.

2 tablespoons Kahlúa
1 tablespoon brandy
1 cup coffee

¼ cup heavy cream, whipped

Pour the Kahlúa and brandy into a mug. Add the coffee and top with whipped cream.

Serves 1

Variation: Instead of 2 tablespoons Kahlúa, use 1 tablespoon Kahlúa and 1 tablespoon crème de cacao. Proceed as directed above.

Hot Drinks Made with Espresso

The following drinks are made with fresh espresso that is still hot. Serve immediately.

Espresso Anisette: A single espresso with 1 teaspoon of anisette added. Serve with a small slice of lemon peel.

Espresso Galliano: A single espresso with 1 teaspoon of Galliano added. Serve with a small slice of lemon peel.

Espresso Kahlúa: A single espresso with 1 teaspoon of Kahlúa added and topped with foam from steamed milk.

Espresso Rum: A single espresso with 1 teaspoon of rum added. Top with whipped cream and a dash of ground cinnamon.

Espresso Whiskey: A single espresso with $\frac{1}{2}$ teaspoon of Irish whiskey added. Top with whipped cream.

Caffè Corretto: A single espresso with $\frac{1}{2}$ teaspoon of grappa added.

Cappuccino Calypso

The coffee-rum taste of this drink is delicious.

*Single espresso
(page 40)*
2 tablespoons Tia Maria

1½ teaspoons rum
3 ounces milk, steamed

Mix all the ingredients except the milk in a glass. Add 1½ ounces steamed milk and 1½ ounces milk foam.

Serves 1

Amaretto-Rum Cappuccino

The almond-cream taste of this drink is sure to satisfy.

*Single espresso
(page 40)*
1½ teaspoons amaretto
1½ teaspoons rum
*1½ teaspoons crème de
cacao*

3 ounces milk, steamed
*¼ cup heavy cream,
whipped*
*Sliced almonds, for
garnish*

Mix the espresso, amaretto, rum, and crème de cacao in a glass. Add 1½ ounces steamed milk and 1½ ounces milk foam. Top with whipped cream and garnish with almond slices.

Serves 1

Brandy-Rum Mochaccino

This drink's chocolate-brandy-rum combination makes it a special one for chocolate lovers.

*Single espresso
(page 40)
1½ teaspoons brandy
1½ teaspoons rum
1½ teaspoons crème de
cacao
1 tablespoon chocolate
syrup*

*3 ounces milk, steamed
¼ cup heavy cream,
whipped
Ground cinnamon
Ground nutmeg
Thin wafer, for garnish*

Mix the espresso, brandy, rum, crème de cacao, and chocolate syrup in a glass. Add 1½ ounces steamed milk and 1½ ounces milk foam. Top with whipped cream, sprinkle with cinnamon and nutmeg, and garnish with a wafer.

Serves 1

Grasshopper Cappuccino

This minty drink is also excellent poured over ice.

Single espresso
(page 40)

1½ teaspoons crème de
menthe

1½ teaspoons crème de
cacao

3 ounces milk, steamed

¼ cup heavy cream,
whipped

Sweetened chocolate
powder

Fresh mint sprig, for
garnish

Mix the espresso, crème de menthe, and crème de cacao in a glass. Add 1½ ounces steamed milk and 1½ ounces milk foam. Top with whipped cream and chocolate powder and garnish with a fresh mint sprig.

Serves 1

Variation: For a Grasshopper Mochaccino, stir 1 teaspoon chocolate syrup into the milk before steaming it or stir the syrup into the espresso before mixing. Proceed as directed above.

Cold Drinks Made with Brewed Coffee

The following drinks are made with cold coffee. Although they are the perfect antidote to a hot summer day, they are delicious any time of the year.

Iced Amaretto–Brandy Coffee

The almond and brandy tastes in this drink complement each other perfectly.

1 ounce amaretto

1 tablespoon brandy

¾ cup coffee

Ice cubes

¼ cup heavy cream, whipped

Sliced almonds, for garnish

Add the amaretto and brandy to the coffee. Pour over ice, top with whipped cream, and garnish with sliced almonds.

Serves 1

Blended Chocolate-Brandy Coffee

Brandy and chocolate combine beautifully to make this a great drink for a warm summer afternoon.

$\frac{1}{2}$ cup coffee

$\frac{1}{2}$ cup milk

2 tablespoons brandy

2 tablespoons chocolate syrup

Ice cubes

Mix all the ingredients together in a blender for 15 to 20 seconds, or until frothy. Pour over ice in a tall glass.

Serves 1

Coffee-Rum Blended

Coffee and rum combine superbly in this smooth-textured cooler.

$\frac{1}{4}$ cup coffee

$\frac{1}{4}$ cup milk

$1\frac{1}{2}$ tablespoons rum

$1\frac{1}{2}$ tablespoons crème de cacao

1 scoop coffee ice cream

Mix all the ingredients together in a blender for 15 to 20 seconds, or until smooth.

Serves 1

Coffee Alexander

The tastes of Kahlúa, amaretto, and chocolate combine to give this drink a real punch.

$\frac{3}{4}$ cup coffee
1$\frac{1}{2}$ tablespoons Kahlúa
1$\frac{1}{2}$ tablespoons amaretto
2 scoops chocolate ice cream

Ice cubes
$\frac{1}{2}$ cup heavy cream, whipped
Sweetened chocolate powder

Mix the coffee, Kahlúa, amaretto, and ice cream in a blender for 15 to 20 seconds, or until smooth. Pour over ice and top with whipped cream and chocolate powder.

Serves 2

Variation: Substitute 2 scoops of vanilla ice cream for the chocolate. Proceed as directed above, topping with a dash of ground nutmeg or cinnamon instead of sweetened chocolate powder.

Cold Drinks Made with Espresso

Unless otherwise specified, the following drinks are made with freshly made espresso and served immediately.

Kahlúa-Rum Chocolate Espresso Float

This cool, sweet treat will melt in your mouth!

Double espresso, cold (page 40)
1 teaspoon Kahlúa
1 teaspoon rum

1 scoop chocolate ice cream
¼ cup heavy cream, whipped
Sweetened chocolate powder

Combine the espresso, Kahlúa, and rum in a glass. Add the ice cream and top with whipped cream and chocolate powder.

Serves 1

Kahlúa–Crème de Cacao Iced Cappuccino

This sweet, creamy concoction is sure to perk you up on a warm day.

Single espresso
(page 40)
3 ounces milk
1½ teaspoons Kahlúa
1½ teaspoons crème de
cacao

Ice cubes
¼ cup heavy cream,
whipped
Ground cinnamon or
sweetened chocolate
powder

Mix the espresso, milk, Kahlúa, and crème de cacao together and pour over ice. Top with whipped cream and cinnamon or chocolate powder.

Serves 1

Cocoa-Mint Espresso Shake

The cocoa-mint combination, mixed with the espresso and vanilla ice cream, makes for a great-tasting pick-me-up.

Single espresso (page 40)
1 teaspoon crème de cacao

¼ teaspoon crème de menthe
1 scoop vanilla ice cream

Mix all the ingredients together in a blender for 15 to 20 seconds, or until smooth.

Serves 1

Iced Brandy–Cointreau Espresso

This drink is just as good using hot espresso.

Double espresso, cold
(page 40)
1 teaspoon brandy
1 teaspoon Cointreau
Ice cubes

¼ cup heavy cream, whipped
Grated orange peel, for
garnish

Combine the espresso, brandy, and Cointreau and pour over ice. Top with whipped cream and garnish with grated orange peel.

Serves 1

Variation: For an Iced Brandy–Crème de Cacao Espresso, omit the Cointreau and substitute 1 teaspoon crème de cacao. Garnish with sweetened chocolate powder instead of grated orange peel.

D i r e c t o r y

W h e r e   t o   G e t   C o f f e e

In addition to your local specialty coffee shop, you can obtain gourmet coffee from the following sources.

Barnie's Coffee & Tea Company
340 North Primrose Drive
Orlando, FL 32803

Has a chain of coffee shops in many states and also sells coffee and related products by mail.

Gloria Jean's Gourmet Coffees
1001 Asbury Drive
Buffalo Grove, IL 60089

Has a chain of coffee shops in many states. Write for the shop nearest you.

Green Mountain Coffee Roasters
33 Coffee Lane
Waterbury, VT 05676

Has a chain of coffee shops throughout New England and also sells coffee and related products by mail.

The Kobos Company
5620 S.W. Kelly Avenue
Portland, OR 97201

Has seven stores in Portland metro area and sells coffee by mail all over the United States.

Second Cup Coffee Company
3300 Bloor Street West, Suite 2900, Box 54
Etobicoke, ON M8X 2X3
Canada

Has a chain of coffee shops throughout Canada. Write for the shop nearest you.

Starbucks Coffee Company
2203 Airport Way South
Post Office Box 34510
Seattle, WA 98124

Has a chain of coffee shops in many states and also sells coffee and related products by mail.

Where to Get Equipment

Your local gourmet or specialty coffee shop may also be a source for coffee-making equipment, or you can obtain information about coffee makers, espresso machines, filters, grinders, and other items by contacting the following manufacturers directly.

Bodum
2920 Wolff Street
Racine, WI 53404

French press and vacuum method coffee makers.

Braun
66 Broadway, Route 1
Lynnfield, MA 01940

Electric coffee makers and home espresso machines, paper and gold filters, coffee grinders.

Coffee Roma
1400 26th Street #101
Vero Beach, FL 32960

Sells espresso machines, stove-top coffee makers to gourmet coffee trade.

Gaggia
Lello Appliance Corp.
355 Murray Hill Parkway
East Rutherford, NJ 07073

Pump and electric home espresso machines, grinders.

Krups
7 Reuten Drive
Closter, NJ 07624

Electric coffee makers and home espresso machines, paper and gold filters, coffee grinders.

Melitta
1401 Berlin Road
Cherry Hill, NJ 08003

Manual and electric coffee makers, stove-top espresso makers, paper filters, coffee grinders.

Pasquini Espresso Company
1501 West Olympic Boulevard
Los Angeles, CA 90015

Electric home espresso machine.

Robert Bosch Corporation
Household Products Sales
2800 South 25th Avenue
Broadview, IL 60153

Electric coffee makers and home espresso machines, gold filters, coffee grinders.

Toddy Products
1513 Gano Street
Houston, TX 77009

Cold-brew coffee maker.

Coffee Organizations

For further information on gourmet coffee, you might want to get in touch with one of these organizations.

National Coffee Association
110 Wall Street
New York, NY 10005

Specialty Coffee Association
One World Trade Center
Suite 800
Long Beach, CA 90831

Index

93